MUCHAS, MUCHÍS RAYAS DE CEBRA

LOTS AND LOTS OF ZEBRA STRIPES

 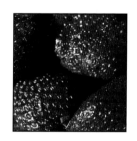 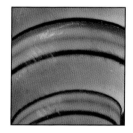

STEPHEN R. SWINBURNE

TRANSLATED BY AÍDA E. MARCUSE

Boyds Mills Press

Honesdale, Pennsylvania

To the marvelous Spassoff boys,
Sebby and Sasha, and to Steffi and Bo,
without whom there would be no marvelous
Spassoff boys.

—S. S.

Los diseños son líneas y formas que se repiten.

Patterns are lines and shapes that repeat.

Algunos diseños son sencillos y algunos no lo son.

Some patterns are simple and some are not.

Puedes encontrar diseños en
You can find patterns in

primavera,
spring,

verano,
summer,

otoño,
fall,

e invierno.
and winter.

Los diseños pueden ser círculos o manchas.

Patterns can be circles or spots.

Los diseños pueden ser rayas o líneas.

Patterns can be stripes or lines.

Los diseños pueden ser espirales.

Patterns can be spirals.

Pueden encontrarse diseños en el pelaje de los animales

Patterns can be found on the fur of animals

o en las plumas de un pájaro.

or the feathers of a bird.

Pueden encontrarse diseños en las escamas de una serpiente

Patterns can be found on the scales of a snake

o en el caparazón de una tortuga.

or the shell of a turtle.

Algunos diseños indican crecimiento.

Some patterns show growth.

Algunos diseños indican la edad.

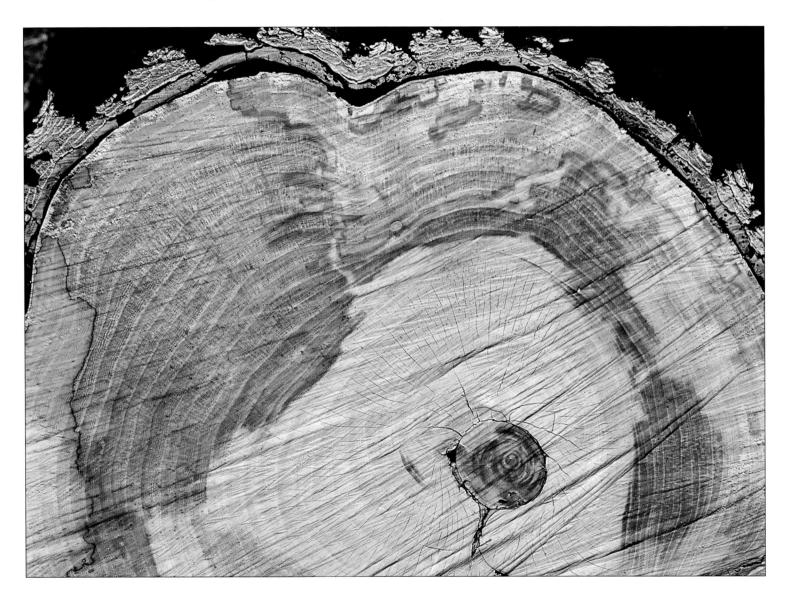

Some patterns show age.

Algunos diseños son líneas rectas.

Some patterns are straight lines.

Algunos diseños son líneas curvas.

Some patterns are curved lines.

Algunos diseños duran poco tiempo.

Some patterns last only a short time.

Algunos diseños duran para siempre.

Some patterns last forever.

Puedes encontrar diseños en un parque,

You can find patterns in a park,

en una laguna,

on a pond,

en la playa,

at a beach,

o en el suelo del bosque.

or on the forest floor.

Encontrar diseños es divertido.

Finding patterns is fun.

Busca los diseños que hay donde vives.

Look for patterns where you live.

¿Puedes encontrar diseños en el bocadillo de tu almuerzo?

Can you find patterns in your lunch snack?

¿Puedes encontrar diseños en las conchas marinas?

Can you find patterns on shells?

¿Puedes encontrar diseños en las verduras?

Can you find patterns in vegetables?

¿Puedes ver diseños en los insectos?

Can you see patterns on insects?

¿Puedes ver diseños en los árboles?

Can you see patterns on trees?

¿Puedes ver diseños en las flores?

Can you see patterns on flowers?

Los diseños hacen de nuestro mundo un lugar hermoso.

Patterns make our world a beautiful place.

Many thanks to the children of Pamela Becker's kindergarten class at the
Brattleboro Central School, Brattleboro, Vermont, and the children of the
West River Montessori School, South Londonderry, Vermont. Thanks, too,
to Wendy Birkemeier, Linda Bailey, Barbara Kouts, Ellen Clyne,
and Advanced Imaging, Manchester, Vermont.

Boyds Mills Press, Inc.
815 Church Street
Honesdale, Pennsylvania 18431
Printed in China

The Library of Congress has cataloged the English hardcover edition as follows:
Swinburne, Stephen.
Lots and lots of zebra stripes : patterns in nature / by Stephen Swinburne.—1st ed.
[32] p. : col. ill. ; cm.
Summary: A photo-essay featuring patterns that appear in nature,
from animal colorings to physical phenomena.
ISBN 1-56397-707-9
1. Nature photography—Juvenile literature. 2. Color of animals—Juvenile literature. 3. Camouflage (Biology)
—Juvenile literature. [1. Nature photography. 2. Color of animals. 3. Camouflage (Biology).] I. Title.
778.9—dc21   1998   AC   CIP
Library of Congress Catalog Card Number 97-77909
Bilingual (Spanish-English) Paperback ISBN: 978-1-59078-633-8
Bilingual (Spanish-English) Hardcover ISBN: 978-1-59078-641-3

First bilingual (Spanish-English) edition, 2008
English edition designed by Stephen Swinburne and Cathy Pernice
The text of this book is set in Garamond.
10 9 8 7 6 5 4 3 2 1